Dr Ryan Anderson

How to raise a boy without toxic masculinity

Contents

    1.

    2.

    3.

Toxic Masculinity

Toxic Masculinity. When you hear or peruse those words, what picture rings a bell; a dominant man or a beta male? My psyche goes directly to the encapsulation of what the ideal man ought to be as indicated by society:

The ideal, strong, fashionable, tasteful, estimated, in every case more spry and smart than the "lesser/more fragile" male. Bond won't ever cry. He's dependably in charge, consistently prepared to battle or f*%k. His feelings skip from quiet to desire from outrage to sex. This ideal... Security... is a sort of "hero" for humanity, keeping the world (or if nothing else England) protected, each battle in turn.

Curiously, when Daniel Craig (a.k.a. the ongoing James Bond) was shot and freely disgraced for wearing his infant in a child transporter, it made me pause and consider how manliness affects humankind. It's no big surprise men are confounded about "how to take care of business." In one breath society says how alluring, endearing, and, surprisingly, provocative it is the point at which a man holds and focuses on his child, and in the following breath society states plainly a "genuine man" doesn't heft his child around.

Right now, the society estimates men against the possibility of the "extremely confident man." The issue is, that this kind of man frequently displays what is presently marked as "harmful manliness." Poisonous manliness is an expression that is getting thrown around recently so we should pause for a minute to attempt to comprehend it a piece better.

I see myself as a current parent, a comprehensive and multifaceted women's activist attempting to bring up youngsters who don't feel tightened by orientation standards or poisonous manliness. In any case, it's challenging to be this sort of parent in a culture that is immersed in assault culture. As a mother, I have many worries for my girl in this world, yet I have an equivalent measure of worries for my child. While my little girl will be shown how to be hyper-watchful in this world to safeguard herself, my child will be informed that young ladies should be shielded from him and his "encourages." My little girl will strike a balance of attempting to be appealing without being excessively provocative while my child should re-think his connections with young ladies while attempting to seem manly enough for other young men. It's every one of them a mystery, one welcomed on by harmful manliness that is so penetrated in our way of life that most guardians simply think of it as a component of fundamental nurturing.

Be that as it may, as reliable guardians who know about the risks of harmful manliness, we attempt to improve. Furthermore, we do so realizing that our endeavours will frequently be gone against by the educational system, different guardians, our youngster's companions, and, surprisingly, other relatives. In any case, we must attempt. Rather than educating our young men that hostility and forceful sexualities are some way or another piece of typical male turn of events, we can rather show them how to successfully impart, how to distinguish and communicate their feelings in solid ways, and how to have a sound comprehension of sexuality that envelops masturbation, assent, and safe sex rehearses.

The possibility that there is just a single method for being anything is ludicrous, yet that is precisely the exact thing harmful manliness is; it is the conviction that to "take care of business" a male must be, areas of strength for forceful, hypersexual and pitiless. What's more, when our milder, gentler young men (a.k.a. non-alphas) can't satisfy the ideal they foster undesirable survival strategies and their confidence drops. The world is needing touchy men.

For this change to occur, I think society necessities to lash out when somebody attempts to disgrace a kid for having a feeling that isn't outrage as we do about our young ladies being physically bothered. What assuming that occurred? What might it resemble on the off chance that moms and fathers began blowing up at any individual who disgraced a male for communicating a "ladylike/more vulnerable" feeling like trepidation, distress, misery, sympathy, or accommodation; indeed, even accommodation. I accept to be an extraordinary pioneer you should know how to follow.

All in all, how would you raise a sort, delicate, caring man who will be sufficiently able to cry and beat someone up if necessary? Or on the other hand delicate enough to quiet his dozing child and genuinely certain enough to endure the jokes thrown at him from his "mates" at work who ridicule him for being an involved parent?

At the point when I make a stride back and take a gander at the gestalt, or the large scale of society, and afterwards take a gander at the miniature (one person), I see two things guardians can do which could drive society to transform each young man in turn.

Be that as it may, showing poisonous manliness isn't a nurturing necessity. All things considered, we can instruct our young men and young ladies that they are equipped for anything. We can overturn the orientation standards that limit them from getting to their maximum capacity as individuals. Let the young men play with dolls; perhaps one day they'll be extraordinary dads. Allow the young ladies to play with building blocks; perhaps one day they'll find successful architects or workers for hire. We can excuse the social thoughts of hostility and undesirable sexuality by having an open exchange about better ways of acting.

We stress over our girls in this world. We do. In any case, harmful manliness is harming our children, as well. Everything we can manage is to educate and display a superior lifestyle choice.

Being characteristically intense, not showing shortcomings, dread or weakness — and not crying no matter what — are qualities that have been boring into the personalities of young men for a long time. While this philosophy is transforming, we have far to go.

What's more, meanwhile, this harmful manliness account can have serious results, both intellectually and genuinely.

At the point when you bottle those feelings they will come out someplace, and possible in unfortunate ways. Young men who have tension or sorrow and can't discuss their sentiments or get the assistance they with requiring can wind up going into enslavement, savagery, self-hurt and at times self-destruction.

Finished suicides are more normal in men than ladies, and at this moment we are seeing crisis division visits and self-destruction at a record-breaking high, particularly between the ages of 10 to 24. We would rather not put this on curbed feelings, yet there is likewise a connection among's harassment and maltreatment toward ladies and not having viable ways of adapting to feelings and disappointments.

Genuinely solid individuals attempt to figure out where their sentiments are coming from. They find out if a specific inclination is aiding or harming them. Recognizing and delivering feelings that are keeping you down is so significant for mental and profound wellbeing.

I've heard the platitude "can't keep those rowdy boys down" frequently yet they won't simply be young men; in the end, they will be developed, men. They will be spouses, fathers, companions, accomplices and associates. Furthermore, it ultimately depends on us to ensure they are great individuals. In any case, how would we bring great men up in a world like this?

I trust the absolute most significant thing that guardians of young men can do to battle this pandemic of harmful manliness is to help our children show feelings and not close off their sentiments.

They needn't bother with being solid consistently. They needn't bother with being in charge. What's more, on the off chance that they aren't in charge, they needn't bother with being embarrassed.

Over the long haul, this turns into a poisonous mix of feelings. Include viciousness, virtual entertainment and the media's cliché depiction of what a fruitful man resembles in the general mish-mash and you can see the reason why we have the issue we have. The cultural strain to continually "take care of business" is bringing about men harming others with a total dismissal of any other individual.

In this way, let your child be miserable, frustrated and hurt. Allow him to cry when he tumbles down the slide and let him know it will be alright regardless of whether they aren't even "truly" hurt. Since these educational encounters and sentiments will direct him and give him that association with others later on. Allow him to open up to you while he's discussing his feelings. Show him compassion. Model it in your regular day-to-day existence.

We can raise great people. We can.

Very much like any kid mother, I have fears and assume weighty liability with regards to bringing up a child. I'm separating my child from the meaning of "harmful manliness" by reminding him he doesn't need to be the most grounded in the class. He is permitted to not be "intense" every so often.

He doesn't necessarily in every case must cover his feelings to show that strength. He doesn't need to be the provider of the most remarkable Money Road leader. He can in any case take care of business and show human articulation. It is alright to not stroll with your chest in the air.

I'm helping him to never put a lady down and to be a partner all things considered. I'm helping him to be nothing similar to those horrendous men we read about in the news.

Thus, here's my recommendation to individual kid mothers all over the place: Backing them when they battle. Maybe this is how we as a whole significantly impact the future — because something needs to change.

Dealing with Emotions

Something happened half a month prior that I will always remember.

I was at the recreation area when I heard a dad shout at his child for crying when he tumbled off the slide. "Quit crying. Strengthen, kid! Try not to be a child!" he shared with his 2-year-old who, to many, would be only that: a child. I wanted to contemplate whether that young man was a young lady, could he treat her the same way? Furthermore, what's the likely long-haul effect of training that kid to stuff his feelings?

As a parent with a degree in brain research and training, I imagined a relationship with my child that elaborate on open discussions about their sentiments and convictions. Now that I have a child, here is a more normal discussion with my child:

Me: "How was your day?"
   Child: "Great"

Me: "What did you do?"

Child: "Stuff."

Indeed, I have had a go at posing explicit inquiries, talking in the vehicle, talking while at the same time strolling, talking in the first part of the day, talking around evening time, on a boat with a goat (you get the float).

My child is an extraordinary youngster — shrewd, entertaining, wise and delicate — yet I stress over him since he keeps everything inside. Sadly, this is valid for so many high school young men. Not every one of them goes to firearms or brutality, however, a considerable lot of them go to medications, liquor, and other hazardous survival strategies to manage their sentiments. So how would we help young men drill down into their sentiments and give them the social close-to-home apparatuses they need to reside in blissful sound lives?

Dispose of orientation generalizations! The obsolete thought that young men should have areas of strength being strong and not helpless or show emotions should be re-composed. Our way of life has done a ton of work somewhat recently to tell young ladies that they can be fearless and solid (there is still work to be finished), however, for young men, the message is still plainly that being delicate is ladylike quality. To give sentiments is an indication of a shortcoming. A kid who cries on the jungle gym may be classified as "a sissy" or "a child." Even good-natured guardians treat young men contrastingly when they tumble down or get injured with messages like "you'll be fine" or "get over it."

As guardians, we can't change society short-term, yet we can do our part to help young men focus on their sentiments. The following are 4 methods for beginning:

1. Urge young men to play with toys and read books that advance "sustaining" and assemble sympathy.

You can in any case purchase your young men's trucks and Legos yet ensure they likewise approach dolls, plush toys, and cooking supplies. Your child will likewise have to know how to cook and shake a child to rest sometime in the not-so-distant future. Fabricate spans with your girl and play casual get-togethers with your child. Urge your child to peruse books with female characters as the principal character. Perusing is one of the most amazing ways of building compassion and by interfacing with both male and female characters, they can investigate both their manly and ladylike side. Boys are viewed as 'normally' unpleasant, however, that is for the most part the result of society's inflexible guidelines around manliness. In this way, responsiveness can be educated to young men. To urge their delicate side to create, offer them the significance of grace while playing with others by sharing their toys and being delicate with pets. Peruse them accounts of extraordinary men in the past who worked for harmony and equity on the planet. Look for open doors locally, for example, a worker coaching program where your young men can work serious areas of strength with models (both male and female) and gain from them. Make sense of for them the significance of placing themselves in the shoes of one more to grasp their torments; it is a beginning in building compassion in your young men. As the expression goes-Showing your kid not to step on the bug is similarly essential to the kid the bug.

Indeed, even in these edified times, young men are frequently expected to smother their tears and swallow their resentment while young ladies are permitted all the more free rein with their feelings. At the point when your child blows up, let him articulate his thoughts, for however long he isn't being damaged or all the way wild.

Then, whenever he's recovered control of his feelings, you can converse with him about the thing he's inclination and why. Assist him with marking his sentiments, whether it's harmed or miserable or irate.

Young men, perhaps more so than young ladies, should be urged to share their feelings. There's a broad assumption that men are solid and don't cry. Young men, and later on developed men, are frequently expected not to show when they've been harmed or on the other hand, as, some they're miserable or told to "suck it up" and to "take it like a man."

Beginning when he's a little child and on up through grade school, urge your kid to communicate how he feels. On the off chance that he's miserable, let him in on it's alright to cry. At the point when he's miserable or apprehensive, cuddle up with him and let him let you know how he feels. If he realizes it's alright when he's young, he's bound to keep on sharing how he feels as he ages. Then, at that point, at some point, ideally, he'll do the same thing with his children.

2. Empower NON-Orientation BASED PLAY

Giving young men an assortment of toys and the valuable chance to participate in non-cliché play assists them with growing up to be balanced. Get him dolls. Playhouse or spruce up with him.

Your child probably won't float towards dolls or a kitchen set, and that is alright, however, offering them offers him the chance for the supporting sort of play that young ladies are presented in overflow. The conventional male/female jobs are turning out to be less ordinary, so presenting young men to an assortment of play at an early age allows them to conclude what they like and could do without given their inclinations and not on old fashioned "customs." And if he favours the pink pots and skillet to activity figures, you may very well have a maturing culinary specialist on your hands!

In the present culture, there are certainly contemplations and convictions about how youngsters ought to play and what they ought to play with. Society, media and toy makers expect young men to play with vehicles, balls and blocks and young ladies to play with dolls, kitchens and spruce-up attire. Youngsters should have chances to play with a wide range of toys and participate in different exercises. We might get various thoughts about what ought to be generally anticipated for play, and we might concur or conflict. The truth of the matter is, that all play prompts higher accomplishment in formative achievements for youngsters who are given the decision of how to play and what to play with.

Be liberal with regards to kids and play. It is extremely proper for young men to play with dolls in the house region and for young ladies to play with blocks and toy trucks. The key is to recollect that play, regardless of which action or toy is utilized, ought to be available to all. Continuously be ready to offer kids decisions in play that incorporate various conceivable outcomes. Try not to consider toys as being orientation explicit, however as suitable for the kid.

Playing with toys, for example, dolls or kitchens can lead youngsters to utilize their minds while fostering their social, close to home and language abilities. These sorts of toys assist kids with figuring out how to collaborate with others and lead straightforwardly to genuine circumstances inside a youngster's current circumstances. Playing in the kitchen drives youngsters to appreciate making food in the kitchen with the grown-ups in their lives. Playing with a doll prompts assisting a youngster with grasping infants, in actuality, and gets ready kids to be within the sight of babies without being terrified of them. Intuitive toys will prompt helpful play and sharing. A movement, for example, "spruce up" likewise prompts fresh out of the plastic new universes for a youngster's creative mind.

Starting play with things, for example, blocks, balls and toy vehicles can prompt an expansion in the engine, language and interactive abilities. Each kid can live it up by playing with blocks. They can utilize their creative mind to make a palace, a carport or a supermarket. Playing with vehicles can lead them to a fanciful outing to the sea and an incredible large truck can convey their #1 things to different regions of the planet. There is no restriction to the creative mind of a kid. Our responsibility is to give them the most potential open doors for them to utilize their minds. Permitting a kid to play with a toy, for however long it's protected and age-fitting, will help them develop and expand their imagination and healthy identity.

Regardless of how you feel about toys and exercises that could conceivably be orientation explicit, remember that all toys can be viewed as sexually unbiased for kids younger than five. Consider permitting a kid to play with toys and dolls. Permit a young lady to play with toy vehicles and blocks. Over the long haul, these open doors are simply going to make them more grounded formatively and all the more balanced when they enter kindergarten. Small kids likewise foster significant fundamental abilities, for example, empathy and regard for others as they enter future formal instructive settings.

3. Never let your kid skip family tasks - it's basic to connect with him in the action, so he can figure out how to assume up liability. This is particularly significant while you're going over everything vital on the most proficient method to bring up a kid youngster as a single parent. Allow him to partake in everything from shopping for food to cooking and housekeeping.

On the off chance that your child disrupts a norm — whether it's utilizing terrible language, missing time limitation, or another infraction — force results.

Young men regard individuals who hold their feet to the fire. After some time he can become unmotivated, and at last ruined and coldblooded.

Treat different grown-ups in your child's life, like educators, mentors and his companions' folks, with deference. Demand that he do likewise. If a contention emerges — say, between your child and his educator — handle what is happening with elegance. Try not to quickly agree with your child, says Gurian. "Hear the two sides of the story, and regardless of whether your youngster is correct, make sense of for him that impoliteness to an instructor is rarely OK," he says. Then say: I'll converse with your instructor to check whether we can determine this. Assuming that something like this reoccurs, I believe you should tell me, and not sass your educator. "You'll show your child critical thinking abilities while stressing regard for other people

For some individuals, particularly men, the two hardest words to say are "Please accept my apologies." Young ladies and ladies frequently are moulded to apologize, whether a conciliatory sentiment is justified. Educating young men on the force of saying "Please accept my apologies" will impart mindfulness and modesty, and give them an early advantage in understanding that assuming individual liability is a quality that will work well for them into their adulthood.

4. Safeguarding and Regarding Young ladies

Around this point, we will generally ponder knights in sparkling defensive layers courageously acting as the hero of a maid in trouble. While that particular situation is old-fashioned, young men coming to the protection of young ladies begin with their singular demonstrations of regard. There certainly exists those circumstances where a man of honour would have to truly or verbally come to the guard of a woman. In any case, exhibiting aware discourse, deflecting eyes when something is unseemly, being aware of spatial limits, and continuously asking before accepting at least for a moment are pragmatic ways that young men can discover that regard for young ladies isn't discretionary.

Since my little honorable man is as yet youthful, we've not proposed a lot of this yet; however, he has figured out how to help keep an eye out for his sisters, to oblige and comprehend that young ladies frequently need to play uniquely in contrast to young men, to never put his hands on a young lady (in his young psyche, this just means messing around together), and to look away from unseemly ads or presentations at the shopping centre.

First of all, when you acquaint your child with new books and Network programs, search for ones with ladies and young ladies as primary characters. Odds are he's now seen bunches of stories with young men at the focal point of the activity.

When young men see men reliably approach ladies with deference, never wondering whether or not to offer help or appreciation, it cultivates those equivalent sensations of sympathy and figuring out in them.

This can be a mate or critical other, mentor, neighbour, a family companion, or some other positive male good examples.

Whenever the situation allows, bring up achievements of ladies in his day-to-day existence and locally. In any event, when you discuss regular stuff, offer remarks like, "Your paediatrician/grandmother/that government official buckled down on this and is a good idea for concocting such smart, wouldn't you say?"

Since again and again ladies don't get acknowledgement for their endeavours, whether it's something physical, profound, or scholarly

Being his friend

Be a Parent First As well as being a friend, I have had very nearly 25 years of working with families. I saw one thing that prompted a ton of trouble between grown-up kids and their folks: when guardians attempted to be their youngsters' companions as opposed to being their folks when they were youthful, particularly during their centre school to secondary school years.

I accept that until a kid turns into a youthful grown-up and starts to develop, the parent's work above all else is to parent, and that means defining limits, giving air to learning and developing and giving the discipline and support an even hand. At the point when this model is followed, it is astonishing the way that a youthful grown-up will ultimately foster sound grown-up fellowship bonds since they comprehend the reason why their folks did how they helped them.

Try to do what a naysayer should do — and Straightforwardness. During that time of bringing up my children, I generally endeavoured to show what I requested from them. We are human, so I bombed on occasion, however that didn't prevent us from proceeding to attempt to live with honesty.

We likewise found that when we were straightforward and conceded our shortcomings and missteps, our kids developed to cherish and regard us for our genuineness and our endeavours to show them a superior way.

In my friend's book, What teenagers want, by Dr Peachy Scotts, she talked extensively about the errors parents of teens make, I recommend it and it's available on the Amazon Kindle store. The main reason I can compose a book like that is if my developed kids won't be shocked by my message, yet approve of why I composed it.

I'm a Christian, so the Holy book is a major piece of my worth framework, yet regardless of what any family's convictions are, nurturing will continuously remember working for a worth framework. Respectability, character and trustworthiness will constantly lead a kid to be a superior grown-up and the most effective way to accomplish that is by reliably attempting to live and lead your family that way.

A parent-youngster bond is one of the exceptional ones on the planet. While some could figure severity and discipline will assist them with bringing up their children better, numerous believe are being their child's companion ought to be given the most extreme significance. Regardless of which classification of guardians you have a place with, you can do the two things simultaneously being your kid's closest companion and raising them well. The following are a couple of ways you can become friends with them:

At times all that a youngster requires is somebody to show up for them. They may be having inconveniences in the everyday schedule by going through something they need to examine with you. Provide them with the window of trust and impart their certainty that they can come and converse with you. In such a manner, gradually and continuously your kid will begin imparting an ever-increasing number of things to you.

I was conversing with one of my associates about our youngsters; he is a lot more seasoned than mine. He had a few extraordinary encounters to pass along. That's what the insight was "companionship, with kids, comes later."

What I assemble from that is the point at which a kid is more youthful, what they need is to be nurtured. Nurturing is instructing, directing, and driving the kid to know how to use sound judgment, to be focused when he/she isn't going with a savvy decision, to be told the best way to cherish self and others, to make companions, and to develop into an insightful youngster.

There are guardians out there who are worried about being their kid's companions. Is testing that if you are, initial, a companion, when the kid is a juvenile or teen, the kid won't require you as a companion. By then, at that point, the individual in question will have companions their age to pay attention to. As teenagers, they need you as a parent, yet they won't let you know that. At the point when you become their companion first, nurturing becomes hard to lay out. The kid may not see you as a power figure, and when you attempt to lay out power, the kid will in all likelihood address you significantly more. That is not the thing you need.

At the point when you are a companion first, it communicates something specific that you believe your kid should like you, to impart to you, and to assist you with feeling associated. On the off chance that that is the situation, that comes down on the kid. Not your kids must assist you with having a decent outlook on yourself. Assuming to that end you are your kid's companion, instead of being his/her parent, then you might have to seek some guidance for yourself. You and your companion (whenever wedded) should zero in on a sound relationship so the lines of nurturing and kinship, even with your kid, can be reevaluated and modified, on the off chance that need be.

At the point when you, the parent, act as a parent, you are establishing a strong starting point for a solid fellowship with your future grown-up kid. There will be many testing times, and nurturing will be troublesome. Indeed, you are fostering a fellowship with your kid in light of how you answer, love, guide, lead, and, mess around

22

with him/her. However, in the early phases of experience growing up, you should be a parent, consistently. Over the long run, the nurturing will change because the kid will require various measures of nurturing.

Here is a model: My child, who will be 1 year old, needs a great deal of nurturing. He's versatile and will get into everything. I should be there to ensure that he isn't getting into anything that will hurt him.

As he progresses in years, I will in any case parent him to ensure he learns and uses sound judgment, yet as he ages, I will have him pursue more choices all alone. At the point when he can dress, I will in any case assist him yet be willing to permit him to settle on choices on what he needs to wear. If he would rather not wear a safety belt, I will uphold that he wears one since that is the law. Nurturing changes when the kid can pursue his own choices, yet you will in any case be there to see that he is settling on solid choices. On the off chance that he doesn't go with the most ideal choice, then he likewise needs to discover that he will have a ramification for that choice.

As you parent, you are establishing the groundwork for companionship later on with your grown-up kid. You are as yet their parent, however when the kid is 18+, it is to a greater degree a companionship with your grown-up kid, and grown-up youngsters will search out nurturing guidance when they need it. At that stage, you can inquire as to whether they believe you should talk as a parent or as a companion.

Think about this: Your kid will have a lot of companions, however just a single parent (two if you are hitched).

How to have that sweet boy?

Each parent needs to bring up kids who are cheerful and effective.

Yet, there's so much nurturing guidance out there.

Who would it be a good idea for you to pay attention to?

Furthermore, which guidance is dependable?

To address those inquiries, I read through many logical articles and exploration diaries.

1. Turn into a more joyful individual yourself.

Close-to-home issues in guardians are connected to profound issues in their youngsters, as made sense of in Raising Bliss. Not just that, miserable individuals are additionally less viable guardians.

Analysts Carolyn and Philip Cowan have additionally observed that cheerful guardians are bound to have blissful kids.

In one concentrate in The Mysteries of Blissful Families, kids were inquired: "Assuming you were conceded one wish about your folks, what might it be?"

Their response?

No, it wasn't so much that their folks would invest more energy with them. Nor was it that their folks would pester them less, or give them more opportunity.

The kids desired that their folks were less worried and tired.

So how might you turn into a more joyful individual? Here is an article with numerous useful ideas.

2. Celebrate as a family, as frequently as possible.

Cheerful families celebrate both the little and large things: the finish of a bustling week, a passing mark, the main day of school, a task advancement, occasions and celebrations.

The festivals can be as straightforward as going to the recreation area together, or as intricate as setting up an impromptu get-together.

Blissful families lead to cheerful kids, so make it a highlight celebration.

3. At the point when your kids converse with you, really focus on them.

Discussing great with your kids is imperative on the off chance that you believe that they should be blissful and effective. One strong method for doing this is to offer them your full consideration at whatever point they address you.

This implies setting te aside your papers and electronic gadgets and truly paying attention to what they need to say.

You'll answer all the more nicely, which will urge your kids to turn out to be more open.

4. Have standard dinners altogether.

Youngsters who have normal feasts with their families become more fruitful in school and in pretty much every region, as made sense of in The Mysteries of Blissful Families.

These kids have bigger vocabularies, more noteworthy self-assurance, and get better grades. They are likewise more averse to drinking, smoking, taking sedates, or fostering mental issues.

And all because these families regularly have dinners together!

5. Help your youngsters to deal with their feelings.

John Gottman's examination demonstrates the way that youngsters who can control their feelings concentrate better, which is significant for long haul achievement. These youngsters even appreciate better actual wellbeing.

To assist your kids with dealing with their feelings, you ought to:

Show profound self-administration yourself
    Understand your youngsters
    Make sense of for your youngsters that all sentiments are satisfactory, yet not all ways of behaving are
    Recognize your youngsters' advancement

6. Guarantee that your youngsters get sufficient rest.
    Research shows that youngsters who get lacking rest:

Have less fortunate mind capability
    Can't concentrate well
    Are bound to become corpulent
    Are less imaginative
    Are less ready to deal with their feelings
    The frightening rundown, right?

To assist your kids with getting sufficient rest, lay out a reliable sleep time routine and cutoff invigorating exercises after supper.

Furthermore, don't permit screen time inside one to two hours of sleep time. This is because the blue light from electronic gadgets influences rests designs and represses melatonin creation.

You can likewise make your kids' room as peaceful and dull as could be expected, to further develop their rest quality.

7. Center around the interaction, not the outcome.

Guardians who overemphasize accomplishment are bound to raise youngsters who have mental issues and take part in hazardous behaviour, as depicted in Raising Satisfaction.

The option in contrast to zeroing in on accomplishment?

Center around the cycle.

So pay special attention to chances to recognize your youngsters' acceptable conduct, mentality, and exertion. As time passes by, they'll normally accomplish improved results.

8. Give your youngsters an additional opportunity to play.

At the point when I say "play," I'm not alluding to the arcade or iPad games. I'm alluding to unstructured recess, ideally outside.

Raising Bliss portrays how recess is fundamental for youngsters' learning and development. The exploration even shows that the less unstructured recess youngsters have, the more probable they are to have formative issues connected with their physical, close to home, social, and mental prosperity.

Having a lively demeanour is even connected to predominant scholastic execution. So give your kids more unstructured recess, and they'll turn out to be better understudies. This forms them into straight-A understudies all alone, however, play is significant for their general turn of events.

9. Urge your kids to keep an appreciation diary.

Keeping an appreciation diary can build your joy levels by 25% over only 10 weeks, as shown by Dr Robert Emmons' examination.

I'm certain the outcomes would have been much more amazing assuming that the term of the review was longer!

Not exclusively were the members who kept an appreciation diary more joyful, they likewise had more expect the future, and they fell debilitated once in a while.

How might you begin keeping an appreciation diary?

Stage 1: Get a scratch pad and pen, and put them on your bedside table.

Stage 2: Consistently before you fall asleep, record a few things that you're grateful for. (Try not to stress over how "enormous" or "little" these things are.)

Here are a few instances of what you could compose:

Great wellbeing
    Adoring family

Delightful nightfall

Delightful chicken stew for supper

Smooth traffic returning

For this, I thoroughly suggest Peach's "31 days of taking care of oneself diary". Got it for my 10-year-old kid and I don't think twice about it. It's available on Amazon.

10. Permit your youngsters to pursue their own decisions (counting picking their discipline).

The Mysteries of Cheerful Families examines a College of California study, which distinguished the advantages of allowing kids to design their timetables and put forth their objectives.

These youngsters were bound to become trained and centred, and pursue more shrewd choices later on.

Allow your youngsters to pick their exercises as well, whenever the situation allows. Dr Rich Gilman found that kids who take part in organized school exercises that they've picked are 24% bound to appreciate going to class.

So as your kid's progress in years, allow them to settle on their very own greater amount decisions. They'll become more joyful and more fruitful subsequently.

11. Resolve the struggles in your marriage.

Youngsters whose guardians have serious conjugal struggles perform more terrible scholastically, are bound to manhandle medications and liquor and are bound to have profound issues, as shown by this concentrate by Kelly Musick.

No curve balls there.

Through my work with understudies, I collaborate with many guardians too. I'm stunned by the number of families in which the guardians have major continuous conjugal issues. (Given my perceptions, I gauge that 30% of these relationships are falling to pieces.)

This most certainly influences the youngsters, who become less persuaded, mindful, and locked in.

On the off chance that you have issues in your marriage that have gone unsettled for months or years, kindly look for help from a specialist or mentor. Your kids - and your marriage - are relying on you.